THE WOODEN HORSE OF TROY

WITHDRAWN

A RETELLING BY
CARI MEISTER

ILLUSTRATED BY
NICK HARRIS

PICTURE WINDOW BOOKS
a capstone imprint

CAST OF CHARACTERS

TROJANS (TROH-junz): people from Troy

GREEKS (GREEKS): people from Greece

HELEN (HEL-uhn): a beautiful Spartan queen, stolen by Paris

MENELAUS (men-uh-LAY-uhs): king of Sparta; husband of Helen

PARIS (PAIR-uhs): a Trojan prince who stole Helen

KING AGAMEMNON (AG-uh-MEM-non): a Greek king and war leader; brother to Menelaus

ODYSSEUS (OH-DIS-EE-uhs): a Greek king; mastermind behind the Trojan Horse

EPEUS (EH-pee-uhs): a friend of Odysseus; builder of the wooden horse

ATHENA (uh-THEE-nah): goddess of wisdom and war

SINON (SY-non): a Greek soldier who tricked the Trojans into taking the wooden horse into the city

LAOCOÖN (LAY-AH-COH-ON): a Trojan man who warned that the wooden horse was a trick

WORDS TO KNOW

OFFERING—to present something as a gift

SACRED—very important or deserving respect; holy objects have to do with religion

SPARTA—a Greek city-state

TEMPLE—a building used for worship

TROJAN WAR—a mythological 10-year battle between the people of Troy and Greece that began when the Trojan Paris stole the Greek Menelaus' wife, Helen

TROY—a city that some believe existed in what is now western Turkey

THOUSANDS OF YEARS AGO,

the Trojans and Greeks fought a war over a beautiful woman named Helen. Helen was married to Menelaus, the king of Sparta, in Greece.

A Trojan prince named Paris fell in love with Helen. She could not resist Paris' handsome face and romantic ways. She, too, fell deeply in love. Secretly, the two of them sailed off together to Troy.

Menelaus was furious at Paris for stealing his wife. He sought revenge. Menelaus asked his brother, King Agamemnon, for help. Agamemnon gathered 1,000 Greek ships full of the best soldiers and sailed for Troy.

But when the ships arrived on Troy's shores, there was a problem. Troy was a walled city. The soldiers could not get into the city to find Helen. Instead, the Greeks and Trojans fought battle after battle on the beaches surrounding Troy.

The battles became known as the Trojan War. The war waged for 10 years. Many people died, but the Greeks still had not been able to get into the city to find Helen—until Odysseus came up with a clever plan.

It had been another long day of fighting, and the smell of blood still hung in the air.

Odysseus wiped the sweat from his forehead. "When will this war end?" he wondered as he removed his armor. "We can't go on this way," he said to himself. "We need to try something new—something clever that will trick the Trojans into letting us into their city."

Odysseus changed his clothes and bandaged his wounds. Then he went out to the fire to see which of his friends had lived through another day.

Odysseus found his friend Epeus by the fire. Epeus was carving a small wooden horse.

"The moon is full tonight," said Epeus. "I bet my daughter is out riding her horse in the moonlight. We used to go together—before the war."

Epeus worked on the horse's mane as Odysseus watched the sparks from the fire dart back and forth.

"It's finished," said Epeus. "It will make an excellent birthday gift for my daughter."

Epeus held up the wooden horse so Odysseus could take a closer look. "Under the horse's belly there's a secret compartment," he said. "I'm going to put a gold coin inside as a surprise."

Epeus paused and looked up at the moon. "Odysseus," he said, "the gods seem to favor you. If I die, will you make sure my daughter gets my gift?"

Odysseus put his hand on Epeus' shoulder. So many of his friends had already died. "Of course I will, Epeus," he said.

That night, with the goddess Athena's help, Odysseus had a dream—a dream that would help end the Trojan War.

In his dream, Odysseus saw Epeus' wooden horse—only this horse could not fit in any saddlebag. This wooden horse was enormous! It stood the height of 10 men. Under the horse's belly was a trapdoor, just like the compartment in Epeus' gift horse.

Odysseus went up through the trapdoor and into the horse's belly. The horse smelled of fresh wood. Inside were benches. Each seat had a man's name carved on it. Odysseus read the names just before he woke.

EPEUS

PHILOCTETES

PHILOCTETES

NEOPTOLEMUS

ODYSSEUS

DIOMEDES

9

Odysseus spent the next day drawing plans of the giant wooden horse. By supper time, he had finished.

Odysseus went in search of Agamemnon. He found the leader in his tent.

"Agamemnon," said Odysseus, "I had a dream. I think Athena must have sent it to me. I believe I have thought of a way to end the war."

Agamemnon raised his eyebrow. "Will it help us get inside the walled city?" he asked. "This war won't end until we get Helen."

Odysseus nodded. "I believe so."

Odysseus left Agamemnon's tent with a smile. He went right to Epeus' tent.

"Epeus," said Odysseus, "I have a job for you. I want you to make a horse just like the one you made for your daughter, with a secret compartment in its belly. But this time, I want you to make a horse that will hold 25 men inside."

Epeus looked puzzled.

Odysseus smiled at his friend. "Your gift horse may be our way to end this war!"

Odysseus explained his plan to Epeus. "When we have finished building the horse, we will pack up camp," he said. "Everyone, except 26 men, will board the boats and sail farther down the coast, out of sight. Twenty-five of us will climb into the belly of the horse. Sinon will remain on the beach, pretending he has been deserted.

Sinon will explain to the Trojans that we had finally wearied of battle and left for home. He'll say we left the horse as a goodwill offering to Athena. The Trojans will pull the horse into the walled city and place it near Athena's temple.

At night, while the Trojans are sleeping, Sinon will signal to the boats that the horse is inside the city's walls. Then, when our soldiers arrive, we will let them in and take the city by moonlight!"

Epeus got started right away. He gathered up the best carpenters and set to work. First the men needed to gather wood for the horse.

"Where are we going to find that much wood?" Epeus wondered. The beach did not have any large trees. There was only one place they could get wood—from their ships.

The soldiers carefully took apart 20 of their wooden ships. They put all the wood into a large pile.

Epeus smiled. "Good work!" he said. "Now we have enough wood for our gift horse!"

The men worked hard. They measured and cut. They figured and hammered. Soon the giant wooden horse was finished.

It was magnificent!

Odysseus gathered the men whose names he had seen in his dream. They climbed into the belly of the wooden horse. They carefully placed their armor and weapons between cloth and wool. When the horse moved they would be silent. Then they sat down to wait.

"Athena, great goddess of war and wisdom," Odysseus silently prayed, "please bring us victory!"

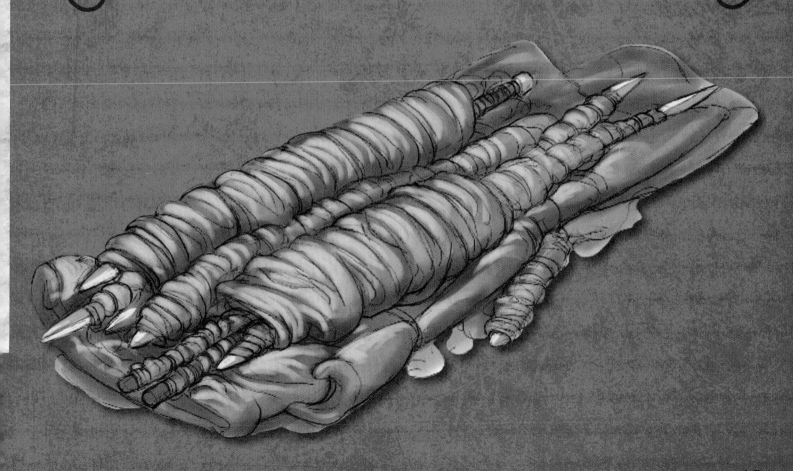

The rest of the men packed up and sailed farther down the coast. Sinon was the only Greek to be seen—Sinon and a large wooden horse. The Trojans watched from the high wall.

"Look!" they shouted. "They're leaving! The war is finally over! But what is that? A horse?"

The Trojans sent out some men to inspect the horse. They found Sinon. "Who are you? What is this?" they asked.

Sinon replied, "My name is Sinon. The Greeks deserted me. They thought I favored your side. This horse is a peace offering to Athena."

The Trojans walked around the horse. "We should bring it into the city!" they said. "We will put it in Athena's temple."

One Trojan, named Laocoön, thought the horse was a trick. "Beware of Greeks bearing gifts," he warned.

But shortly after he said this, two giant snakes emerged from the sea and ate him.

The Trojans decided it was best not to listen to Laocoön.

"It's the will of the gods for us to accept this offering," said the Trojans.

They opened the city gates and wheeled the giant horse into Athena's temple.

Odysseus and his men were finally inside the city. But they had to be still and wait.

That evening the Trojans had a big party. They were happy the war was over. They ate and drank. They laughed and danced into the night. Eventually exhausted, they went home to bed.

When the Trojans were asleep, Sinon took a ladder, opened the horse's trapdoor, and let out Odysseus, Epeus, and the other Greek warriors.

Odysseus shook Sinon's hand. "Good work, Sinon! They believed you! Now go to the gate and let in the rest of our soldiers!"

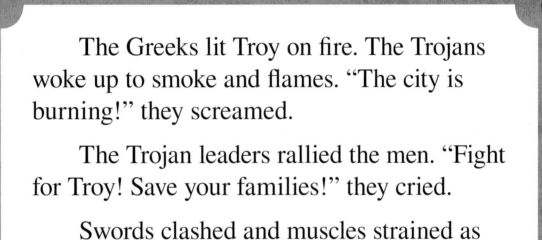

The Greeks lit Troy on fire. The Trojans woke up to smoke and flames. "The city is burning!" they screamed.

The Trojan leaders rallied the men. "Fight for Troy! Save your families!" they cried.

Swords clashed and muscles strained as the bloody battle wore on into the morning.

The Trojans fought bravely, but the Greeks had caught them unaware. The wooden horse had worked. The Greeks had won the war, and the beautiful Helen was returned to Menelaus.

The Greeks took what they wanted from the ruined city. Odysseus' men robbed Athena's sacred temple. Athena became angry. She determined that Odysseus and his men should suffer by wandering the seas for 10 long years.

While Odysseus was destined to sail for many years, the gods blew Epeus' ship home with great speed. Epeus was able to present his daughter with the gift horse himself.

"He's lovely, Father!" she said.

Epeus looked up at the sky. "Thank you, Odysseus," he whispered.

READ MORE

Fontes, Justine, and Ron Fontes. *The Trojan Horse: The Fall of Troy.* The Exchange. Carmel, Calif.: Hampton-Brown, 2007.

Kelly, Sophia. *What a Beast!: A Look-It-Up Guide to the Monsters and Mutants of Mythology.* Mythlopedia. New York: Scholastic, 2010.

Namm, Diane, retold by. *Greek Myths.* Classic Starts. New York: Sterling, 2011.

INTERNET SITES

FactHound offers a safe, fun way to find Internet sites related to this book. All of the sites on FactHound have been researched by our staff.

Here's all you do:

Visit *www.facthound.com*

Type in this code: 9781404866706

Super-cool stuff! Check out projects, games and lots more at www.capstonekids.com

LOOK FOR ALL THE BOOKS IN THE GREEK MYTHS SERIES:

THE BATTLE OF THE OLYMPIANS AND THE TITANS

JASON AND THE ARGONAUTS

MEDUSA'S STONY STARE

ODYSSEUS AND THE CYCLOPS

PANDORA'S VASE

THE WOODEN HORSE OF TROY

Thanks to our adviser for his expertise and advice:
Terry Flaherty, PhD
Professor of English
Minnesota State University, Mankato

Editor: Shelly Lyons
Designer: Alison Thiele
Art Director: Nathan Gassman
Production Specialist: Sarah Bennett
The illustrations in this book were created digitally.

Picture Window Books
1710 Roe Crest Drive
North Mankato, MN 56003
877-845-8392
www.capstonepub.com

All books published by Picture Window Books are manufactured with paper containing at least 10 percent post-consumer waste.

Library of Congress Cataloging-in-Publication Data
Meister, Cari.
The wooden horse of Troy / a retelling by Cari Meister; illustrated by Nick Harris.
    p. cm. — (Greek myths)
  ISBN 978-1-4048-6670-6 (library binding)
  1. Trojan horse (Greek mythology)—Juvenile literature.
I. Title.
  BL820.T75M45 2012
  398.20938'02—dc22
                                    2011006987

Printed in the United States of America in North Mankato, Minnesota.
122011   006505R